A Little Less NOISE

by Barry Louis Polisar

illustrations by David Clark

I Don't Wanna Go to School

I don't wanna go to school," Tom said to his mommy.
You know you have to go to school," Mom said back to Tommy.
"No one likes me there," said Tom. He hid beneath the covers.
"I'd rather stay in bed," he said. "Grow up," said Tommy's mother.

Tom ducked his head beneath the sheets and kicked his feet about.
His mother heard him whimpering and told him not to pout.
"I just can't face another day, the children are not nice."
She wiped his cheek and told him to follow her advice.

"But people laugh at me at school," Tom told his mom again.
"The teachers will not talk to me. I don't have any friends."
"Now Tom get up," said Tommy's mom. She hoped he was convincible.
"You've got to go to school," she said, "because you are the Principal."

Our Dog Bernard

Our dog Bernard lived in the back yard
'Til one warm summer day.
Our dog Bernard hit the boulevard;
He just up and ran away.

He left a note taped to the door
"I'm tired of this life," it said.
"I'm tired of eating dog food
And getting chased off of the bed."

He ran off with the bus driver,
He's living with her now I'm told.
Spends all his time watching TV,
Getting fat and growing old.

Oh Bernard, Bernard, please come back,
You know that I love you.
I'll let you ride in the four-wheel-drive.
I'll make it all up to you.

The Skatter-Brack Flath Who Lives in my Bath

I think I'm pretty lucky, I'm sure you'll agree,
'Cause in my house there's a bath tub you see
And in that tub lives a Skatter-Brack Flath
Who won't let me take a shower or a bath.
I grab my robe, my soap and towel;
I hear a shriek and a deep, deep howl.
When Dad tells me, "get in the bath,"
I tell him all about the Skatter-Brack Flath.

He's as real as the Gutchum Gee-Gillie Gah-Ged
Or the Bottom-Bo, Bitty-Bree, Slock-Slo Sled
Or the Slotum-Slaw Silklie-See Sap-Sucking Sool
Who want me at home when I should be in school.
Or the Google Nosed Liddy Lap Licking La-Lude
Who never lets me finish all of my food.
Or the Gobbin Go Gittie-Gatch Gitchie-Gap Goo....
And you better watch out—so they don't get you!

I Wanna Be a Dog

I wanna be a dog, wanna wag my tail,
Dump garbage cans, race cars and vans,
Bite the man who brings the mail.

I wanna be a dog, wanna lie on the floor,
Chase squirrels and cats, get fed, get fat,
Chew your shoes and bark at the door.

I wanna be a dog, wanna dig big holes,
Sniff trees and ground and basset hounds
And pee on telephone poles.

I wanna be a dog, wanna roll in the dirt,
Wanna run in the street, get mud on my feet
And jump up onto your shirt.

I wanna be a dog, wanna drool all around,
Scratch fleas and ticks; run after sticks,
I just wanna be a hound.

I wanna have dog breath, wake the neighbors, too.
I'll lick your hand, be the best friend to man;
I've got nothing better to do.

I wanna be a dog, I want my nose to be wet.
Don't need a pedigree; all I wanna be
Is somebody else's pet.

I'm a Three-Toed, Triple-Eyed, Double-Jointed Dinosaur

I'm a three-toed, triple-eyed, double-jointed dinosaur
With warts up and down my back.
I eat shiny automobiles, tow-trucks and airplanes,
I love to munch on railroad tracks.

I sleep all day, at night I play,
Some say I am well read;
I eat two or three libraries for breakfast
And they go right to my head.

Factories are good for snacks,
I love that red hot steel.
And you know we need our supply
Of iron in our meals.

I love burnt toast, raw fish, rump roast,
Buttered asparagus, too.
But the thing that I like most to eat
Is little kids just like you!

I'm a three-toed, triple-eyed, double-jointed dinosaur
With warts up and down my back.
I eat shiny automobiles, tow-trucks and airplanes,
I love to munch on railroad tracks.

My Brother Threw Up on My Stuffed Toy Bunny

My brother threw up on my stuffed toy bunny,
You better not laugh 'cause it really isn't funny.
It was lying in my bed while I was sound asleep
But it could have been worse—it could have been me.

My bunny's name was Bill and he was pink and white,
His eyes were purple and they glowed at night.
His ears were ragged and his nose was red,
He was soft as my pillow from his paws to his head.

My Dad tried to help when I started to scream.
He threw my bunny in the washing machine.
But my bunny, Bill, still smelled so bad;
I lost the best friend that I ever had.

So bunny now sits on my shelf at home,
Next to my smelly toy telephone
And the dirty old bear with the stains and the spots,
'Cause my little brother throws up a lot.

My brother threw up on my stuffed toy bunny,
You better not laugh 'cause it really isn't funny.
It was lying in my bed while I was sound asleep
But it could have been worse—it could have been me.

I've Got a Dog and My Dog's Name is Cat

I've got a dog and my dog's name is Cat,
Bet you never heard anything as crazy as that.
But not only that, I've got a cat
And my cat's name is Dog, like my dog's name is Cat.

I bet you think that's pretty absurd—
But wait 'til you hear about my fish, Bird.
And listen to me and you'll hear this:
I've got a bird and I call him Fish.

With my bird and my fish, my dog and my cat,
People all stare when I tip my hat.
It's strange as can be when we walk in the park,
But it's stranger still when the cat starts to bark.

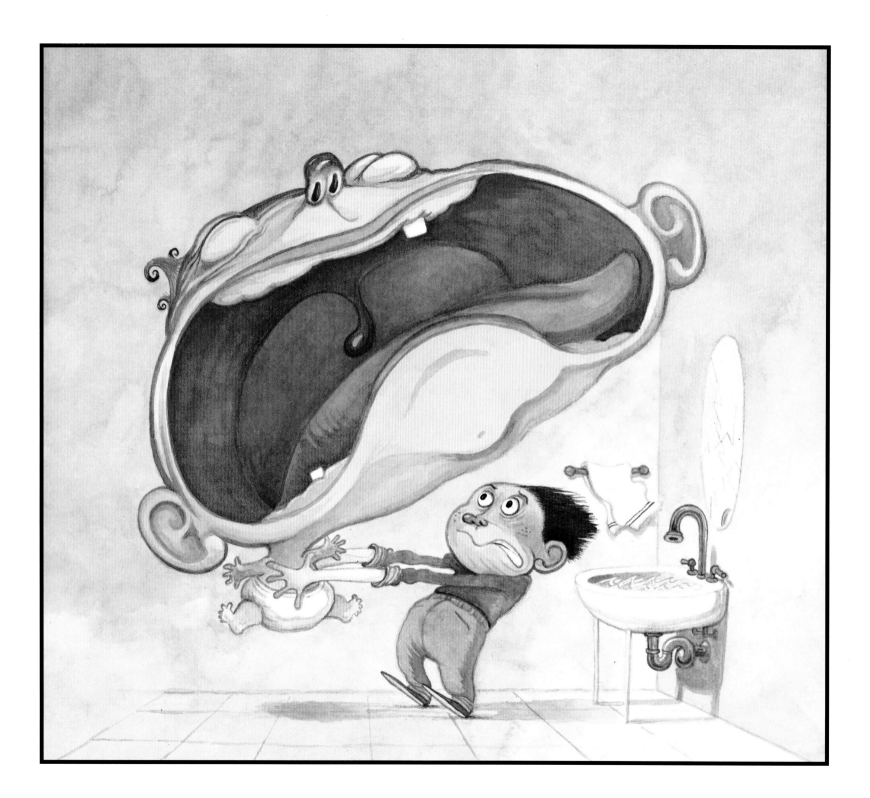

Go and Hush the Baby

"Go and hush the baby," was what my Mommy said,
The baby was crying; I thought she'd wet her bed.
I went into the baby's room, said, "Baby, don't you cry."
But baby didn't listen so I sang a lullaby.
I bounced her in my arms, I sat her in a chair.
I caught her almost every time I threw her in the air.

But baby kept on crying, I couldn't make her stop,
I tried to make her burp, but baby just would not.
I thought perhaps I'd wash her—her smell was hard to stand.
I grabbed my nose and changed her clothes; that's how it all began.
I was washing baby when baby disappeared,
I don't know how it happened; I just know that it sounds weird.

A hand came up from in the pipe and pulled her down the drain,
And now it seems that baby will not be seen again.
There is no trace of baby now—there is no residue,
Just a piece of broken soap and a bottle of shampoo.
I think my mom and dad will yell—they'll tell me I'm so bad;
To think I lost another one—oh boy, will they be mad!

I Lost My Pants

I lost my pants—has anybody seen them?
I can't go anywhere 'til they return.
I can't go to school like this; I know they'll send me home;
Being naked is my concern.

My pants disappeared last night while I was sound asleep;
They slipped away so silently, they didn't make a peep.
I wonder where they went to? I wish they'd come back soon.
I want my slacks to walk right back and sit down in my room.

This happens all the time—last week it was my gloves,
After that my hat, then the jacket that I love.
Dad won't help me look for them. You know what he said?
"All your clothes are rumpled up and dumped beside your bed."

I left them here just yesterday when I went to bed—
And here they are, I found them; just like my daddy said.
Now finally I can do whatever I may choose.
I can even go to school again....if I can find my shoes.

I've Got a Teacher, She's So Mean

I've got a teacher, she's so mean,
She never laughs, she always screams,
She says, "Pay attention and do what I said,"
But if you ask me, she's crazy in the head.
She makes me nervous, she makes me squirm,
She says, "All teachers must be firm."

She always calls on me when I don't raise my hand,
So I answer her in ways that she can't understand.
She says, "What is the answer to number two?"
I say, "Ock nock ditty wok, dickie pickie poo."
She says, "Don't be funny, you'd better get it right."
I say, "Shimmie, Gimmie Galla Gillie, tacky ticky tite."

She never lets us laugh, she never lets us smile,
"Wipe that grin off your face, you're acting just like a child."
It's, "Work, work, work—no late papers today."
She's tired of excuses and yells at us all day.
She doesn't like children, she doesn't like kids,
Likes only regulations and you know I never did.

I never see her laughing, she's so strict,
She never believes me when I say I'm feeling sick.
She doesn't think it's funny when I fall off my chair,
And everybody knows that she's really unfair.
She can't understand me and I've got it made;
But I know she really loves me 'cause I'm still in first grade.

He Eats Asparagus, Why Can't You Be That Way?

Whenever I am naughty, whenever I am bad
Whenever I do something that makes my parents mad
(Like the time I bit the mailman or left stuff on the floor)
My parents say, "Why can't you be like the boy who lives next door?"

He always makes his bed and he always eats his food
He likes his itty, bitty sister and he's never ever rude,
When I don't eat what's on my plate my parents both will say,
"He eats asparagus, why can't you be that way?"

He is never dirty, he always takes a bath,
He loves to do his homework too, especially math.
At school he is an angel, he always sits up straight,
He's always very helpful and he never comes in late.

He always says, "I'm sorry," "Excuse me," "Thank you," "Please,"
He always dresses nicely, not like me.
He's never spilt his milk, lost a glove or slammed a door,
Stuck out his tongue or giggled in school or left things on the floor.

He goes to bed at nine each night and brushes all his teeth,
And Mommy wishes I was him and that he was me.
I've never even seen him burp, he does what he is told,
But the boy next door is thirty four years old!

When the House is Dark and Quiet

Late at night when Mommy and Daddy have gone out,
Me and my brother get to scream and jump and shout,
'Cause the house is dark and quiet and we're left all alone
With another teen-age baby-sitter talking on the phone.
We tip-toe on our tip-toes and we listen to her laugh,
While the water is running, so she thinks we're in the bath.
She tells her friend she's hungry, so we know just how to tease her;
We go and get the kitty cat and hide it in the freezer.

Cindy opens up the door, you should have seen her leap,
Then we tell her, "That's the place where the kitty always sleeps."
She starts yelling and sends us both to bed,
But Tim and me don't listen to a single thing she's said.
Convinced that Tim and I are finally lying sound asleep,
She settles on the sofa and turns on the TV,
So Tim sneaks to the basement to disconnect the fuse,
While I'm up in the attic, thumping in my father's shoes.

While Cindy checks the TV set, examining the plug,
I crawl across the living room, underneath the rug.
We stand up on the sofa with carrots up our noses,
Pretending we are monsters—not wearing any clothes-es.
Cindy says she won't come back, just like Mike and Sue
Melody and Barbara, John and Linda, too.
Mom and Dad can't leave us now, although they feel they must,
But we can't understand why no one wants to stay with us.

My Mother Ran Away Today

My mother ran away today
She walked right out the door,
Packed her tooth brush and pajamas
Said, "I can't take it any more."

She said that she was tired,
She said she had her fill
Of cooking our meals, washing our clothes
And cleaning up all our spills.

She said she'd write us letters
With no return address,
She said she'd come back someday
But now she has to rest.

She took the plants, she took the cats,
Took our pictures from the wall,
And though it's just been two hours,
I wish that she would call.

I never thought I'd miss her,
Isn't that the way?
You never know how much Mom means to you,
Until she runs away.

Underwear

Underwear is everywhere but mostly underneath.
Usually you can't see what goes on beneath
Ragged clothes, evening gowns or the finest three-piece suit.
Underwear is everywhere; there is no substitute.

Everyone is equal when it comes to underwear,
Because beneath your underwear it's just yourself that's there.
Everyone wears underwear—or at least they should.
Underwear is lots of things, but mostly it is good.

Some like the feel of cotton. I share this belief.
Likewise I don't like boxer shorts, give me a pair of briefs.
Some don't like to talk about it, that's because they're shy.
People laugh at underwear, but I do not know why.

"Now don't use bleach on underwear." That's what my mom will say.
" 'Cause bleach will eat the fabric and soon they'll wash away."
Underwear with lots of holes, is a sorry sight,
Look around and try to see who's wearing their's too tight!

Underwear is everywhere but mostly underneath.
Usually you can't see what goes on beneath
Ragged clothes, evening gowns or the finest three-piece suit.
Underwear is everywhere; there is no substitute.

Don't Put Your Finger Up Your Nose

Don't put your finger up your nose,
'Cause your nose knows that's not the place it goes.
You can sniffle, you can sneeze,
But I'm asking you—please—
Don't put your finger up your nose.

Don't stick your finger in your ear,
'Cause then your ear will find it hard to hear.
You can thump and you can tug it,
But please don't plug it—
Don't stick your finger in your ear.

Don't put your finger in your eye,
That's not a thing I think you oughta try.
You can blink it, you can wink it,
But I don't think it
Would be good to put your finger in your eye.

And don't stick your finger down your throat.
'Cause that will just make you start to choke.
Then up will come your dinner
And you'll start to look much thinner,
So don't stick your finger down your throat.

Don't put your finger up your nose,
'Cause your nose knows that's not the place it goes.
You can sniffle, you can sneeze,
But I'm asking you—please—
Don't put your finger up your nose.

The poems in this book were originally published as songs—many over twenty-five years ago. They first appeared in book form as song lyrics with accompanying music in my songbook, *Noises From Under the Rug.* That book is now out-of-print.

Transforming these songs to poems was relatively painless, thanks in large part to my cousin, Sheldon Biber, who has been much, much more than an editor over the years. Cousin Shelby not only introduced me to a love of poetry and encouraged me to write when I was younger, but fueled my love of music and listened to my early songs, urging me to go public. This book is dedicated to Sheldon; my rainbow still has many of his colors running through it.

My wife, Roni, also deserves much thanks; she read, re-read and fine-tuned these selections and helped me keep a balance between my revisions and my original work. Roni has always kept me in tune.

Barry Louis Polisar, 2000
Rainbow Morning Music

Published by Rainbow Morning Music
2121 Fairland Road
Silver Spring, MD 20904

isbn # 0938663-23-2

First Edition